The red lines show Clara's astonishing
tours of Europe with the captain, both by
land in a horse-drawn wagon and by sea.

For Ethan

CLARA

The (Mostly) True Story of the Rhinoceros Who Dazzled Kings,
Inspired Artists, and Won the Hearts of Everyone . . .
While She Ate Her Way Up and Down a Continent!

Emily Arnold McCully

schwartz & wade books · new york

early three hundred years ago, when half the world was still a mystery to the other half, a Dutch sea captain arrived in India and called on an old friend. As they were trading stories, a remarkable creature padded into the room.

"What on earth is that?" cried Captain Van der Meer.

"Our rhinoceros," said his host.

"My, she is strange!" the captain exclaimed.

"She's an orphan," said his friend. "We call her Clara."

Gazing at the creature, the captain had an idea. *In Europe, people believe that rhinos are mythical beasts. Surely they will pay to see a real one. I could give up my lonely life at sea.*

And so the captain offered to buy Clara.

"But how will you care for her?" his friend asked. "She eats a great deal."

Van der Meer admitted he didn't know. "But I will sort it out," he promised.

Clara was hoisted slowly onto Van der Meer's ship. It must have been frightening, but she trusted the captain.

"Good girl," he said, and secured her so that when the vessel pitched she would not be hurled into the water.

The crew was delighted to have a new passenger.
There were already a few animals on board, to provide
everyone with milk, eggs, and companionship.

Clara gave everyone she liked a lick.
Her tongue was as soft as velvet.
  She ate stacks of hay and drank
gallons of water.
  She adored oranges and beer.

But after only two days, Clara seemed unhappy. The captain realized she was drying out in the sun. He gazed at the heaving sea. . . .

Fish! He could apply a daily slathering of fish oil to Clara's hide to keep her moist.

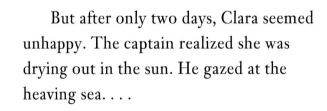

As the ship rounded the Cape of Good Hope, Van der Meer fleshed out his plan.
He would travel from town to town with Clara, selling tickets to all who wanted to see
her. Of course, he would need to buy a great deal of hay. He had taken on a very large
responsibility—but he was finding his rhino to be a pleasant companion.

Before Clara's hoofs touched dry land in Holland, word had spread that a mythical beast was in the harbor. An excited crowd gathered to meet the ship.

Van der Meer hurried Clara off to his home in Leiden.

Now the captain had to figure out how to transport his Clara on her grand tour. He drew a design for a wagon and hired some shipbuilders to build it. It would take a team of eight horses to pull her.

Meanwhile, Clara went on eating. She was gaining twenty pounds a day and was always agreeable. When things didn't go well—as when work on the wagon went too slowly—Van der Meer looked deep into his rhino's eyes and felt calm. Clara might have been homely on the outside, but she had a beautiful soul.

The captain had posters and flyers printed:

THERE HAS ARRIVED IN EUROPE AN ANIMAL CALLED
RHINOCEROS. SHE HAS SKIN LIKE SEASHELLS, EARS LIKE
AN ASS, CAN SWIM LIKE A DUCK, AND IS AS TAME AS A DOVE.
SHE EATS 100 POUNDS OF HAY AND 30 LOAVES OF BREAD A DAY
AND DRINKS 14 BUCKETS OF WATER AND BEER.

At last, the unlikely duo were ready to start their adventure. To Van der Meer's delight, a little horn had sprouted on Clara's forehead.

The captain sent word of his real mythical beast to Frederick the Great, the king of Prussia. When they rolled into Berlin, the king met them at the fish market, where Clara could be treated with oil of sardine.

"*Unglaublich!* Incredible!" the king exclaimed. "What a monstrous creature—and yet how noble!" Van der Meer was very pleased. Frederick had recognized Clara's essence.

Frederick gave the captain a bag of gold coins to buy enough hay, beer, and oranges for the next leg of their journey.

Off they went to Vienna, where Empress Maria Theresa
pronounced Clara "*Herrlich!* Magnificent!"

Then back to Germany. In Regensburg, Freiburg, and Dresden, Clara was drawn, painted, and modeled in porcelain.

"*Schrecklich!* Frightful!" people exclaimed. "And yet what a beautiful spirit!"

Clara's horn itched as it grew, so the captain gave her a board to rub against. She ate and ate and drank and drank.

Every week, she was weighed and measured. "Five thousand pounds, eleven and a half feet around, six feet high," the mayor of Leipzig announced.

Van der Meer had a bigger wagon built.

When Clara had been on the road for a year, Frederick II
of Hesse invited her to his orangerie.

"She must be happy," the captain remarked. "And when Clara
is happy, so am I."

Onward. Near Mannheim, they ran into a problem. The steep, narrow, rocky roads would not support a rhinoceros-carrying wagon. The glittering Rhine River beckoned. Could Clara be persuaded to board a raft? And if it capsized, could a rhinoceros really swim?

While Clara munched grass, loggers felled trees and lashed them together. The captain called, "Come, my Clarakin," but she ignored him. Out came a basket of oranges—

and onto the raft went Clara.

What a sight they were! Years later, people would say that seeing Clara had changed them forever. The captain knew just what they meant.

But as Clara's celebrity grew, so did she. It became impossible to pay for all her food. Sometimes the captain went hungry so Clara could eat.

They crisscrossed Germany, went home to Leiden, then left again, finally heading to France. Surely the richest king in Europe, Louis XV, owner of two lions, two tigers, a pelican, a camel, and a seal, would pay handsomely to meet the strangest animal on earth.

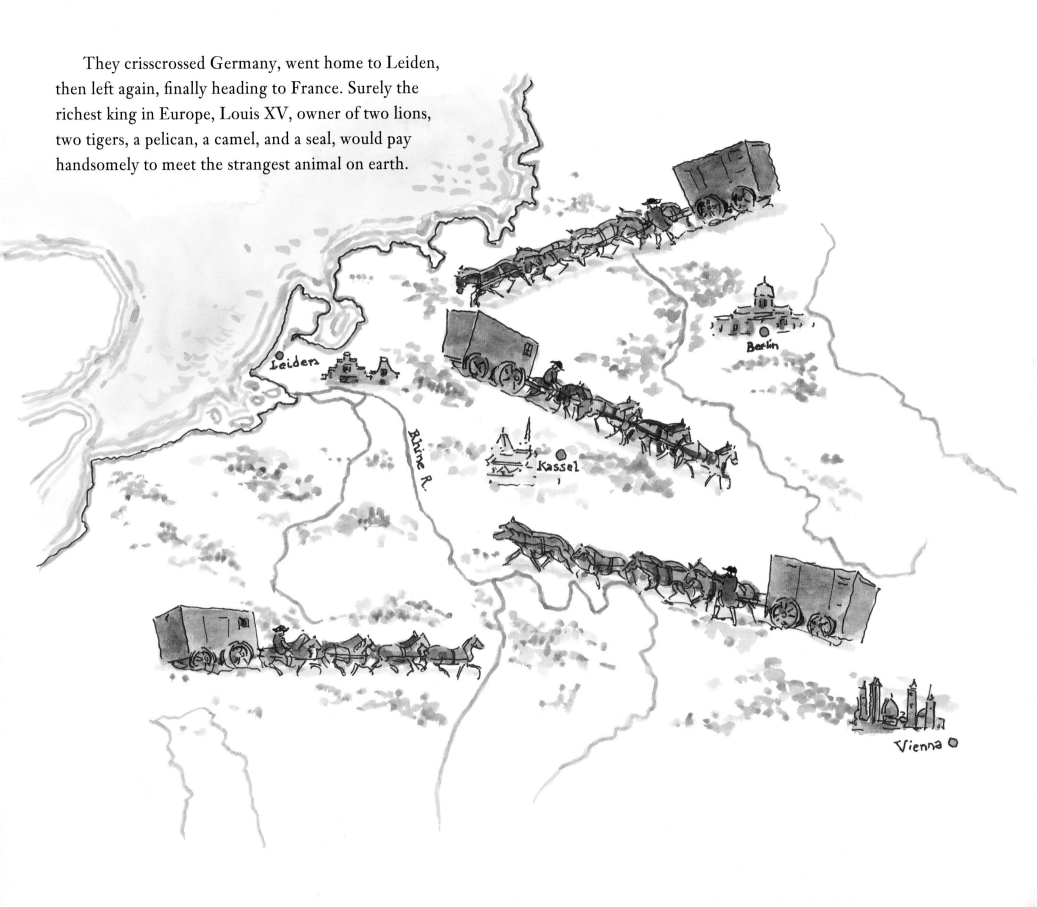

When Clara arrived at the Palace of Versailles, the king looked her over from top to bottom. Clara munched the royal lawn.

At last, he said, "She is a marvel. I want her for my menagerie."

The captain was speechless. Sell his beloved Clara? Unthinkable!
Still, if he let her go, Clara could retire in comfort at Versailles.
"You may have her for one hundred thousand gold pieces," he said at last.

Louis, who had expected the rhinoceros as a gift, dismissed him in a huff.

Van der Meer crumpled with relief. "Oh, Clarakin, I nearly lost you!" he cried.

But she still had to be fed. Where would the money come from?

Luckily, Paris went absolutely wild for Clara.
At the Saint-Germain Fair, peasants, merchants,
tradesmen, aristocrats, and royalty lined up to
gaze into her soul. Van der Meer charged extra for
private viewings and for stroking Clara's soft lip.

Poets wrote verses, and painters made portraits. Scientists came to examine her, and her picture appeared in Diderot's famous *Encyclopedia*. Musicians composed songs in her honor.

Hairdressers created the style *à la rhinocéros*, and chic women
everywhere copied it. Gowns *à la rhinocéros* were worn to balls. In salons,
people spoke of nothing else. The French navy even christened a new ship
La Rhinocéros. It was Rhinomania!

Rome would not be outdone by Paris! Clara rolled on to Italy and triumphed again.

Then, one morning, Clara looked different. Her horn had fallen
off. Could she be sick?

The captain was about to cancel Clara's appearances, but when he
looked into her eyes, he was reassured. It was clear that she loved this
life. "Sweet Clarakin," he told her, "we will carry on."

So Clara went to Venice. Venetians, too, saw her nobility, horn or no horn.
And one day, a little knob appeared on Clara's forehead: she was growing a new horn!
Soon it was bigger than the first.

For seventeen years, Clara charmed audiences
all over Europe.

When the end came, the pair were in London.
Clara's trusting eyes had grown cloudy.

Van der Meer put his face close to hers and she gave
him a lick. He knew she was dying.

The captain had kept his promise to take care of her,
no matter what. And she had taken care of him, too.
They had lived a whole lifetime together.

"Dear Clarakin," he murmured, "you've been the
greatest trouper and my truest friend."

For a moment, Clara seemed to be remembering it
all. And then she shut her eyes.

AUTHOR'S NOTE

Carting a three-ton rhinoceros all over Europe in a horse-drawn wagon seems absurd . . . but it really happened. It is a unique chapter in the long history of human relations with animals—one that completely captivated me.

Today, we know that confining and exhibiting a wild animal is inhumane. But Clara lived in a time before people understood her needs. The captain adopted and cared for her as well as he could, and the Europeans who saw a rhino for the first time were moved by her majesty.

We know what Clara looked like (Captain Van der Meer commissioned broadsides, posters, and souvenir medals, and artists made portraits) and the routes she traveled. I imagined the rest. I believe that over their seventeen years together, Clara and the captain became deeply attached.

Clara was born around 1740, and her mother was killed soon after her birth. Since baby rhinos depend on their mothers for about two years, she was helpless when Jan Albert Sichterman, a director of the Dutch East India Company in Assam, took her into his house. He and his family treated her like a spoiled pet, even letting her eat off the china. By the time Douwe Mout van der Meer, a merchant marine, met and adopted Clara during a visit to his friend in 1741, she was too tame to live in the wild. The captain became like a mother to her, and in his care, Clara lived far longer than any other rhinoceros taken from its native environment.

A rhino's stomach can tolerate almost any plant, but it is not efficient at absorbing nutrients. So Clara had to take in much more food than her body actually needed—over 100 pounds per day! She ate constantly. (Note the piles of poop in Pietro Longhi's painting.) Her thick, tough skin hung in folds that disguised the underlying shape of her body. Her only hair was her eyelashes, ear fringes, and tail brush.

Clara's itinerary was astonishing, and at times it might have been grueling—she traveled to Hanover, Berlin, Leipzig, and several other German cities, as well as Vienna, Paris, Marseilles, Naples, Rome, Bologna, Venice, London, and beyond. Her arrival in cities, towns, and royal courts created feverish excitement among people of every station and walk of life, from kings to peasants to philosophers to artists. One German broadsheet says that she died in London on April 15, 1758, but no newspaper reported this momentous event. So Clara's end is a bit of a mystery.

For centuries, Indian rhinoceroses ranged over all of the North Indian Plain and into China. They have always been relentlessly hunted, as Clara's mother was. Today, approximately three thousand remain, primarily on preserves in Bhutan, Nepal, and India. The population has recovered somewhat from its low of about two hundred.

Three hundred years ago, Clara was an astonishing curiosity. Seen in the flesh, this sublime creature inspired awe. By so patiently and agreeably posing for the public, year after year, Clara seemed to ask that humans strive to understand the creatures who share our world. Today, we know that we must also cherish and protect them.

Pietro Longhi, *Exhibition of a Rhinoceros at Venice*, 1751.

Great thanks to Glynis Ridley, whose marvelous book *Clara's Grand Tour* introduced me
to Clara, and to Elizabeth Hess, author of *Nim Chimpsky: The Chimp Who Would Be Human*,
who gave me invaluable insight into the ethical treatment of wild animals.

RESOURCES

arttattler.com/archiveoudry.html

forteantimes.com/features/articles/4603/a_rhinoceross_tale.html

Holmes, Mary Tavener. *My Travels with Clara*. Los Angeles: Getty Publications, 2007.

nationalgallery.org.uk/paintings/pietro-longhi-exhibition-of-a-rhinoceros-at-venice

Ridley, Glynis. *Clara's Grand Tour: Travels with a Rhinoceros in Eighteenth-Century Europe*. New York: Grove Press, 2005.

sanmartin-artscrafts.com/2014/03/clara-rhinocerosnotes.html

The text of this book is set in Archetype.
The illustrations were rendered in pen-and-ink and watercolor on Arches paper.

MANUFACTURED IN CHINA

2 4 6 8 10 9 7 5 3 1

First Edition

The green line in the inset below shows Clara's first sea voyage with the captain from her home in Calcutta, in India, to Rotterdam, in Holland.

CLARA'S
TOURS

1741–1758

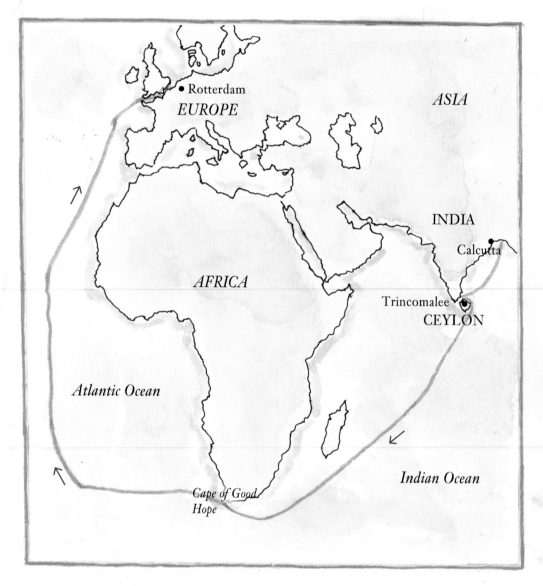

Rotterdam
EUROPE

ASIA

INDIA
Calcutta

AFRICA

Trincomalee
CEYLON

Atlantic Ocean

Indian Ocean

Cape of Good
Hope